The Cambodian Campaign during the Vietnam War: The History of the Controversial Invasion of Cambodia and Laos

By Charles River Editors

A picture of American planes bombing Cambodia

About Charles River Editors

Charles River Editors is a boutique digital publishing company, specializing in bringing history back to life with educational and engaging books on a wide range of topics. Keep up to date with our new and free offerings with this 5 second sign up on our weekly mailing list, and visit Our Kindle Author Page to see other recently published Kindle titles.

We make these books for you and always want to know our readers' opinions, so we encourage you to leave reviews and look forward to publishing new and exciting titles each week.

A picture of American choppers over Cambodia

Introduction

"When elephants fight, ants should stand aside." - Norodom Sihanouk, King of Cambodia, on the

Vietnam War

"People usually refer to the bombing of Cambodia as if it had been unprovoked, secretive U.S. action. The fact is that we were bombing North Vietnamese troops that had invaded Cambodia, that were killing many Americans from these sanctuaries, and we were doing it with the acquiescence of the Cambodian government, which never once protested against it, and which, indeed, encouraged us to do it. I may have a lack of imagination, but I fail to see the moral issue involved and why Cambodian neutrality should apply to only one country. Why is it moral for the North Vietnamese to have 50,000 to 100,000 troops in Cambodia, why should we let them kill Americans from that territory, and why, when the government concerned never once protested, and indeed told us that if we bombed unpopulated areas that they would not notice, why in all these conditions is there a moral issue?" - Henry Kissinger

The Vietnam War could have been called a comedy of errors if the consequences weren't so deadly and tragic. In 1951, while war was raging in Korea, the United States began signing defense pacts with nations in the Pacific, intending to create alliances that would contain the spread of Communism. As the Korean War was winding down, America joined the Southeast Asia Treaty Organization, pledging to defend several nations in the region from Communist aggression. One of those nations was South Vietnam.

Before the Vietnam War, most Americans would have been hard pressed to locate Vietnam on a map. South Vietnamese President Diem's regime was extremely unpopular, and war broke out between Communist North Vietnam and South Vietnam around the end of the 1950s. Kennedy's administration tried to prop up the South Vietnamese with training and assistance, but the South Vietnamese military was feeble. A month before his death, Kennedy signed a presidential directive withdrawing 1,000 American personnel, and shortly after Kennedy's assassination, new President Lyndon B. Johnson reversed course, instead opting to expand American assistance to South Vietnam.

Over the next few years, the American military commitment to South Vietnam grew dramatically, and the war effort became both deeper and more complex. The strategy included parallel efforts to strengthen the economic and political foundations of the South Vietnamese regime, to root out the Viet Cong guerrilla insurgency in the south, combat the more conventional North Vietnamese Army (NVA) near the Demilitarized Zone between north and south, and bomb military and industrial targets in North Vietnam itself. In public, American military officials and members of the Johnson administration stressed their tactical successes and offered rosy predictions; speaking before the National Press Club in November 1967, General Westmoreland claimed, "I have never been more encouraged in the four years that I have been in Vietnam. We are making real progress...I am absolutely certain that whereas in 1965 the enemy was winning, today he is certainly losing." (New York Times, November 22, 1967).

At the same time, the government worked to conceal from the American public their own doubts and the grim realities of war. Reflecting on the willful public optimism of American officials at the time, Colonel Harry G. Summers concluded, "We in the military knew better, but through fear of reinforcing the basic antimilitarism of the American people we tended to keep this knowledge to ourselves and downplayed battlefield realities . . . We had concealed from the American people the true nature of the war." (Summers, 63).

By the end of 1967, with nearly half a million troops deployed, more than 19,000 deaths, and a war that cost $2 billion a month and seemed to grow bloodier by the day, the Johnson administration faced an increasingly impatient and skeptical nation. Early in 1968, a massive coordinated Viet Cong operation - the Tet Offensive - briefly paralyzed American and South Vietnamese forces across the country, threatening even the American embassy compound in Saigon. With this, the smiling mask slipped even further, inflaming the burgeoning antiwar movement. Although American soldiers didn't lose a battle strategically during the campaign, the Tet Offensive made President Johnson non-credible and historically unpopular, to the extent that he did not run for reelection in 1968. By then, Vietnam had already fueled the hippie counterculture, and anti-war protests spread across the country. On campuses and in the streets, some protesters spread peace and love, but others rioted. In August 1968, riots broke out in the streets of Chicago, as the National Guard and police took on 10,000 anti-war rioters during the Democratic National Convention. By the end of the decade, Vietnam had left tens of thousands of Americans dead, spawned a counterculture with millions of protesters, and destroyed a presidency, and more was still yet to come.

As the results of the Tet Offensive made clear, American forces were hamstrung by political constraints and a wide range of self-imposed limitations, and the United States struggled to deal with the greater strategic nimbleness of the North Vietnamese during the late 1960s. The tremendous power of the American military, blending technological strength and professional skill, gave the Americans the advantage in many, though of course not all, tactical encounters. On the strategic and operational level, however, the North Vietnamese held many of the trump cards. Constrained by a heavily defensive strategy, the U.S. found itself mostly forced to respond to the North's initiatives, and a reactive strategy placed even an extremely potent combatant at a severe disadvantage.

The North Vietnamese, on the other hand, fought a war of conquest motivated by a form of imperialistic communism. After ruthlessly imposing their Marxist creed on the north's population and butchering those who resisted, Ho Chi Minh's cadres and their successors pursued victory against South Vietnam without qualms or restrictions. Though often outmatched on the battlefield by their American opponents, they pursued victory by any and all means, untroubled by the objections of conscience and unrestrained by the public opinion of their subjugated citizenry. The North Vietnamese understood clearly the weaknesses of America's relative restraint, its defensive stance, and its increasing domestic anti-war movement. They exploited these advantages to the full, guided by one principle: winning.

One of their prime strategic advantages lay in their use of Cambodia. Cambodia, headed by the effective quisling King Norodom Sihanouk, officially adopted a stance of neutrality. This neutrality represented a sham, however. Sihanouk permitted the North Vietnamese Army (NVA) and the Viet Cong (VC) to operate on Cambodian territory. He did so out of fear of North Vietnam and in the hope that the North Vietnamese would not attack him while he attempted to deal with the Khmer Rouge.

The NVA and Viet Cong used this favorable situation to create numerous bases just across the Cambodian border from South Vietnam, enabling them to launch attacks and then retreat to their "neutral" refuge where the U.S. usually refused to authorize its troops to follow them. As U.S. Secretary of State Henry Kissinger said, "Washington had convinced itself that the four Indochinese states were separate entities, even though the communists had been treating them as a single theater for two decades and were conducting a coordinated strategy with respects to all of them." (Shaw, 2005, 3).

Furthermore, the North Vietnamese developed a shortened supply route through Cambodia to lessen dependence on the partially compromised Ho Chi Minh Trail traversing Laos. Sihanouk allowed Hanoi to use the deep water port of Sihanoukville to bring weaponry and supplies in from ships sailing out of communist China, from where the Viet Cong moved them the short distance to the South Vietnamese border, along the so-called Sihanoukville Trail, without fear of American interdiction.

This strategic situation changed briefly, however, during the 1970 Cambodian Campaign, when American and South Vietnamese forces crossed the border into Cambodia and brought the battle to the previously immune enemy there.

The Cambodian Campaign during the Vietnam War: The History of the Controversial Invasion of Cambodia and Laos looks at the secret mission and the manner in which it roiled American sentiment at home. Along with pictures depicting important people, places, and events, you will learn about the bombing of Cambodia like never before.

Contents

The Tet Offensive

By the start of 1968, the United States had been heavily invested in opposing Vietnamese communism for the better part of two decades, and with the benefit of hindsight, the American war effort that metastasized there throughout the 1960s may seem like a grievous error and a needless waste of blood and treasure on an unwinnable and strategically insignificant civil conflict in a distant, culturally alien land. Indeed, it is still difficult for Americans today to comprehend how it was that their leaders determined such a course was in the national interest. Thus, it is essential at the outset to inquire how it was that a succession of elite American politicians, bureaucrats, and military officers managed, often despite their own inherent skepticism, to convince both themselves and the public that a communist Vietnam would constitute a grave threat to America's security.

Vietnam's first modern revolution came in the months of violence, famine, and chaos that succeeded World War II in Asia. Along with present-day Laos and Cambodia, the country had been a French colony since the late 19th century, but more recently, at the outset of World War II, the entire region had been occupied by the Japanese. Despite the pan-Asian anti-colonialism they publicly espoused, Japan did little to alter the basic structures of political and economic control the French had erected.

When Japan surrendered and relinquished all claim to its overseas empire, spontaneous uprisings occurred in Hanoi, Hue, and other Vietnamese cities. These were seized upon by the Vietnam Independence League (or *Vietminh*) and its iconic leader Ho Chi Minh, who declared an independent Democratic Republic of Vietnam (DRV) on September 2, 1945. France, which had reoccupied most of the country by early 1946, agreed in theory to grant the DRV limited autonomy. However, when the sharp limits of that autonomy became apparent, the Vietminh took up arms. By the end of 1946, in the first instance of what would become a longstanding pattern, the French managed to retain control of the cities while the rebels held sway in the countryside.

Ho Chi Minh

From the outset, Ho hoped to avoid conflict with the United States. He was a deeply committed Communist and dedicated to class warfare and social revolution, but at the same time, he was also a steadfast Vietnamese nationalist who remained wary of becoming a puppet of the Soviet Union or the People's Republic of China. Indeed, Ho's very real popularity throughout the country rested to no small extent on his ability to tap into a centuries-old popular tradition of national resistance against powerful foreign hegemons, a tradition originally directed against imperial China. As such, he made early advances to Washington, even deliberately echoing the American Declaration of Independence in his own declaration of Vietnamese independence.

Under different circumstances, Americans might not have objected much to a communist but independent DRV. The Roosevelt and Truman administrations had trumpeted national independence in Asia and exhibited almost nothing but contempt for French colonial rule. However, as Cold War tensions rose, and as the Soviet Union and (after 1949) Communist China increased their material and rhetorical support for the Vietminh cause, such subtle gradations quickly faded. Considering the matter in May 1949, Secretary of State Dean Acheson asserted that the question of whether Ho was "as much nationalist as Commie is irrelevant. All Stalinists in colonial areas are nationalists . . . Once in power their objective necessarily becomes subordination [of the] state to Commie purpose." (Young, 20 – 23).

Acheson

Compared with their predecessors in World War II and Korea, the average American soldier in Vietnam was considerably younger and in many cases came from more marginal economic backgrounds. The average American soldier in World War II was 26, but in Vietnam, the average soldier was barely 19. In part, this was due to President Johnson's refusal to mobilize the national reserves; concerned that calling up the National Guard would spook the public and possibly antagonize the Russians or Chinese, Johnson relied on the draft to fill the ranks of the military.

In all, between 1964 and 1973, fully 2.2 million American men were drafted into the military, and an additional 8.7 million enlisted voluntarily, or at least semi-voluntarily. Knowing that draftees were more likely to be assigned to combat roles, many men who expected to be drafted took the initiative to enlist in the military before the Selective Service Board had a chance to call them up. This was a risky bet, perhaps, but not necessarily a crazy one, because enlistees were less than half as likely as draftees to be killed in Vietnam.

Moreover, given the numerous Selective Service deferments available for attending college, being married, holding a defense-related job, or serving in the National Guard, the burden of the draft fell overwhelmingly on the people from working class backgrounds. It also particularly affected African Americans.

The American military that these young draftees and enlistees joined had been forged in the crucible of World War II and were tempered by two decades of Cold War with the Soviet Union. In terms of its organization, equipment, training regimens, operational doctrines, and its very outlook, the American military was designed to fight a major conventional war against a similarly-constituted force, whether in Western Europe or among the plains of northeast Asia. As an organization, the military's collective memories were of just such engagements at places like Midway, Normandy, Iwo Jima, Incheon, and the Battle of the Bulge. These campaigns predominately involved battles of infantry against infantry, tanks against tanks, and jet fighters against jet fighters. As boys, many of the young men who fought in Vietnam had played as soldiers, re-enacting the heroic tales of their fathers and grandfathers. The author Philip Caputo, who arrived in Vietnam as a young marine officer in 1965, recalled, "I saw myself charging up some distant beachhead, like John Wayne in *Sands of Iwo Jima*, and then coming home with medals on my chest." (Caputo, 6).

Expecting a simple conflict of good against evil and knowing little to nothing of the local culture, American soldiers in their late teens and early twenties arrived in Vietnam and found a world of peril, privation, and moral ambiguity. Despairing of and for young rookie soldiers like Caputo, Bruce Lawler, a CIA case officer in South Vietnam, virtually exploded with rage: "How in hell can you put people like that into a war? How can you inject these types of guys into a situation that requires a tremendous amount of sophistication? You can't. What happens is they start shooting at anything that moves because they don't know. They're scared. I mean, they're out there getting shot at, and Christ, there's somebody with eyes that are different from mine. And boom—it's gone." (Saltoli, 177).

Indeed, with a few notable exceptions, the American military experience in Vietnam consisted largely of small-scale encounters. Understanding full well that contesting a conventional battle with the better-armed Americans amounted to committing suicide, the Viet Cong waged an asymmetrical guerrilla-style campaign that capitalized on their superior knowledge of the terrain, their closer relations with local villagers, and their deeper commitment to the cause. Viet Cong guerrillas wore no uniforms, did not always bear their arms openly, did not observe traditional battle lines, and blended in with the villagers who supported them. During the war, an American soldier was as likely to be killed by a land mine, a booby trap, or a hidden sniper as by an enemy he could see.

To the Viet Cong themselves, such tactics were natural and justified in a "people's war": "The soldiers came from the people. They were the children of the villagers. The villagers loved them, protected them, fed them. They were the people's soldiers." (FitzGerald, 201). To the Americans, however, the insurgents seemed sneaky and treacherous, readier to hide behind women and children than to stand and fight like men.

Of course, such guerrilla tactics served to blur the lines between combatant and civilian. As Specialist 4th Class Fred Widmer of Charlie Company explained, "The same village you had gone in to give them medical treatment . . . you could go through that village later and get shot at on your way out by a sniper. Go back in, you wouldn't find anybody. Nobody knew anything . . . You didn't trust them anymore." (Widmer).

Faced with such a determined opponent, skilled in asymmetrical warfare and enjoying considerable popular support, General William Westmoreland chose to fight a war of attrition. While he did employ strategic hamlets, pacification programs, and other kinetic counterinsurgency operations, he largely relied on his massive advantage in firepower to overwhelm and grind down the Viet Cong and NVA in South Vietnam. The goal was simple: to reach a "crossover point" at which communist fighters were being killed more quickly than they could be replaced. American ground forces would lure the enemy into the open, where they would be destroyed by a combination of artillery and air strikes.

Westmoreland

Naturally, if American soldiers on the ground often had trouble distinguishing combatants from civilians, B-52 bombers flying at up to 30,000 feet were wholly indiscriminate when targeting entire villages. By the end of 1966, American bombers and fighter-bombers in Vietnam dropped about 825 tons of explosive every day, more than all the bombs dropped on Europe during World War II. As Secretary of Defense Robert McNamara wrote to President Johnson in May of 1967, "The picture of the world's greatest superpower killing or seriously injuring 1,000 noncombatants a week, while trying to pound a tiny backward nation into submission on an issue whose merits are hotly disputed, is not a pretty one." (Sheehan, 685).

The apparent stalemate of 1967 was not only a concern for the Americans. In Hanoi, Ho Chi Minh's war council debated its own strategy for driving the Americans and their allies from the south. In 1966, the party had agreed to pursue "decisive victory in a relatively short time." (Duiker, 263). However, their aggressive battlefield operations over the succeeding year - combined actions of both southern Viet Cong guerrilla cadres and units of the North Vietnamese Army spirited south along the Ho Chi Minh Trail - proved largely ineffective against the combined forces of the South Vietnamese Army and the increasing numbers of American troops in the Military Assistance Command, Vietnam (MACV). In the words of one Communist general, "In the spring of 1967 [MACV commander General William] Westmoreland began his second campaign. It was very fierce. Certain of our people were very discouraged. There was much discussion of the war—should we continue main-force efforts or should we pull back into a more local strategy. But by the middle of 1967 we concluded that [the Americans and South Vietnamese] had not reversed the balance of forces on the battlefield. So we decided to carry out one decisive battle to force LBJ to de-escalate the war." (Arnold, 9)

The ensuing Tet Offensive of 1968, during which the militant faction of the North Vietnamese government launched a massive attack on South Vietnam, intended to rouse a popular rebellion but instead resulted in the near-extermination of the Viet Cong and heavy losses to the NVA. In many large and small-scale actions, the Americans and South Vietnamese turned the tables on their opponents and crushed them. In just one incident at Binh An in 1968, the 3rd Squadron, 5th Cavalry engaged the NVA K14 Battalion to such effect that the surviving North Vietnamese jumped into the sea in an effort to escape. Major Michael D. Mahler's account serves almost as a microcosm of the unexpected devastation of communist forces during Tet: "We had once more stumbled into a situation and been able to turn it to our advantage. But it was more than stumbling and it was not luck that brought success. It was soldiers in hot steel vehicles out in the glaring sand looking and poking until the enemy, North Vietnamese and Viet Cong, never knew when or where an armored column would crop up next." (Starry, 2002, 147).

By the time the siege of Khe Sanh was lifted in April 1968, the initial Tet Offensive had been repulsed throughout South Vietnam. Indeed, in many American accounts, the end of fighting at Khe Sanh is identified as the final action of the Tet Offensive. To the North Vietnamese, however, the "general offensive, general uprising" of Tet was a longer-term project that would continue at least through September. In the words of Tran Van Tra, while the initial offensive had failed to spark a widespread popular uprising or significantly weaken allied military capacity, it had nonetheless "sent shudders throughout the enemy's vital points, and destabilized its military, political, and economic foundations throughout South Vietnam," creating an opportunity for North Vietnam to "continue strong assaults and compensate for . . . earlier shortcomings in order to win even bigger victories." (Werner and Huynh, 48).

Nonetheless, the troops who carried out the initial offensive had suffered heavy casualties. This was particularly true of the local Viet Cong guerrillas, who had made up the bulk of the Communist forces in the south. These networks of disciplined and highly-motivated guerrilla cadres had survived for years in the face of the American and South Vietnamese militaries by keeping to the shadows and avoiding large-scale pitched battles. In that sense, the initial Tet attacks granted General Westmoreland and his officers exactly what they had long wished for: traditional pitched battles against the VC. The result had been as bloody as it was predictable, with an overwhelmingly lopsided body count and the decimation of Viet Cong networks throughout South Vietnam. A continued offensive would require massive reinforcements. Thus, through March and April, perhaps as many as 90,000 NVA reinforcements were sent down the Ho Chi Minh Trail to infiltrate the South.

Nonetheless, from the perspective of American policymakers, the "Mini-Tet" attacks made a bad situation even worse. They kept Vietnam in the headlines and helped to convince a growing number of Americans that the war was fundamentally unwinnable. During the earliest days of the Tet Offensive, Americans naturally responded to the Communist offensive with a wave of patriotism and belligerence, and in early February, a national poll reported that fully 55% of Americans supported increasing America's military commitment to defeating Communism in South Vietnam. However, the steady drip of violent stories and images that came out during the first half of 1968 effectively soured that initial burst of confidence and defiance, further eroding Americans' already shaky confidence in their leaders and the war they had chosen to fight.

There is no more significant instance of this sea change in public opinion than the very public agony of CBS newsman Walter Cronkite. Cronkite's conversion from supporter to outspoken war skeptic—simultaneously a cause, an effect, and a microcosm of the larger national reassessment—did not come easily. While his doubts about the war effort had multiplied in the years preceding Tet, he had been hesitant to abandon his public stance as an objective journalist:

President Johnson allegedly responded to Cronkite's report with the comment, "If I've lost Cronkite, I've lost middle America." Reflecting on events much later, Cronkite himself was surprised by the impact of his commentary, and particularly its effect on the president: "I didn't expect it to be that effective It should have shocked the President only if he didn't know the full scale of the thing himself" (Willenson, 196).

Cronkite in Vietnam

Indeed, despite some claims to the contrary, the ferocity and scope of the Tet Offensive appeared to have come as a massive shock to both the military command and the Johnson administration. Diplomat Richard Holbrooke, a member of the Johnson White House's Vietnam group who had earlier been an assistant to U.S. Ambassador Henry Cabot Lodge, Jr. in Saigon, recalled, "There was an enormous confusion in the period from January 30, 1968, to March 30, 1968. Notwithstanding all the memoirs that have been written claiming that intelligence predicted the Tet offensive, the simple fact is that the Tet offensive caught the Administration unprepared. That's a fact." (Willenson, 149 – 50).

Under the circumstances, then, it is hardly surprising that American press coverage of the Tet Offensive and its fallout grew increasingly cynical, mistrustful of authority, and pessimistic. Even among historians and observers who believe that the prevailing narrative of the Tet Offensive has been badly misguided, and that it was actually a strategic victory for the Americans and South Vietnamese, it is generally acknowledged that the press response was at the very least an understandable reaction to the excessive optimism of the administration before the campaign.

In such a poisonous, confused atmosphere, official claims of an American victory in the Tet Offensive, whatever their merits, were bound to ring hollow. As Vermont Senator George Aiken declared, "If this is a failure, I hope the Viet Cong never have a major success." (Olson and Roberts, 186).

The Prelude to Bombing Cambodia

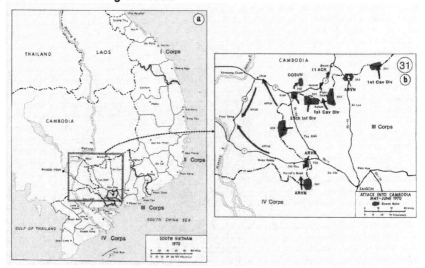

An American military map of the border between Cambodia and Vietnam

Following the Tet Offensive, General Creighton Abrams took over command from General Westmoreland. Abrams, who won notoriety as a skilled, highly aggressive lieutenant colonel in the 4th Armored Division during World War II, changed the focus of American effort in Vietnam. He instituted the practice of "Vietnamization," which would eventually enable the United States to disentangle itself from the conflict; replaced "search and destroy" with pacification; and shifted focus to interdicting North Vietnamese logistics.

Abrams

Ironically, while Abrams' new strategy appeared to focus on "hearts and minds" and increasing American detachment from the struggle, the third element – attacking NVA logistics – opened the door to one of America's most successful large-scale offensives during the war, one which might actually have produced victory if pushed through to its conclusion rather than aborted due to extraordinary opposition from the press and from a group of senators led by Edward Kennedy.

As for Vietnamization, North Vietnamese negotiator Le Duc Tho demolished the notion with ruthless logic during talks with Henry Kissinger in Paris: "All too acutely, he pointed out that our strategy was to withdraw enough forces to make the war bearable for the American people [...] He then asked the question that was also tormenting me: 'Before, there were over a million U.S. and puppet troops, and you failed. How can you succeed when you let the puppet troops do the fighting? Now, with only U.S. support, how can you win?'" (Coleman, 1991, 213).

The new strategy began laying the groundwork for the offensive even before it reached the planning stages. Cambodia's king, King Norodom Sihanouk, and his family profited personally from the NVA and Viet Cong presence in their country, renting the communists a fleet of trucks with which they transported a river of weaponry and materiel from Sihanoukville to the South Vietnamese border. Hanoi, which would have eventually disposed of Sihanouk, no doubt thought of the quote, actually an improved version of a clumsy statement by Vladimir Lenin, that "the capitalists will sell us the rope with which we hang them."

Rob C. Cross' picture of Sihanouk

The Americans now realized that the Sihanoukville trail and infiltration across the Cambodian border represented an equal or larger threat than the Ho Chi Minh Trail in Laos. In late 1969 and into the first months of 1970, they began major operations in War Zone C along the border with Cambodia, trying to cut the numerous enemy supply and infiltration trails in that area. Units involved included the U.S. 11th Armored Cavalry. The Americans sent numerous armored squadrons into the area, consisting of M113 ACAVs, APCs with upgraded armor, and M551 Sheridan light tanks. The Sheridan, an interesting armored vehicle with a M81E1 Rifled 152 mm Gun which could also fire MGM-51 Shillelagh missiles in addition to shells, proved effective and lethal in the jungle environment despite its technical quirks and occasionally troublesome electronics.

The Sheridan

A Sheridan and mine clearing team operating in Cambodia

The armored squadrons each deployed extensive "traplines" of ingeniously rigged Claymore anti-personnel mines and other explosive devices each time they set up a perimeter near a North Vietnamese trail. The M18A1 Claymore mine fired a blast of 700 1/8-inch steel balls in one chosen direction, with an optimal killing range of 50 yards. Though designed to be detonated by a hand control connected to a detonation wire, the GIs set up the mines for detonation by tripwire instead.

The "Blackhorse" (11th Armored Cavalry) and other units soon learned their jungle environment well, with its stifling heat, thick vegetation, and the characteristic red dust of the roads and trails. They also acquired extensive practical knowledge of the NVA and Viet Cong's tactics, which they put to good use in setting up their Claymores in elaborate patterns to carefully turn trails and alternate routes into death traps. This type of warfare represented a battle of wits, one the Americans frequently won. As Captain Sewall Menzel of the 11th Armored Cavalry's 2nd Battalion remarked, "The automatic ambush caught the imagination of the average trooper. Individuals would spend hours thinking of and discussing new ways with which to turn the trick and trump the Viet Cong. It is [...] a systematic means by which the enemy's freedom of movement can be severely curtailed and even paralyzed. [...] The results are incontrovertible." (Nolan, 1990, 14).

The use of these techniques did indeed interfere strongly with NVA infiltration into Tay Ninh Province. Besides killing many hundreds of communist soldiers, the Americans intercepted large quantities of rifles, other man-portable weapons, ammunition, and countless tons of rice along the Cambodian border trails.

At the same time, the style of warfare represented a grueling, physically and mentally demanding struggle, of small groups of men stalking each other through the stifling, humid jungle darkness. The severely outnumbered Americans needed to "circle the wagons" with their vehicles at night and remain on extreme alert to avoid being overrun and slaughtered by sudden night attacks. For their part, the Vietnamese faced the constant fear of being blown to pieces by Claymores and other booby traps. In most cases, both sides met the situation with grim determination.

All the while, the American soldiers could not, of course, pass the invisible barrier of "neutral" Cambodia's frontier. In fact, their orders strictly forbade them to even fire back across the border if shot at from the other side, meaning that all operations occurred beyond typical effective weapon ranges of the demarcation. While the Americans carried out occasional "illegal" bombing raids and other incursions in Cambodia, for the most part they adhered to their self-imposed hamstringing until the Cambodian Campaign. Oddly, Sihanouk did not even protest the American bombing sorties, because, as he explained, "it is in one's own interest, sometimes, to be bombed – in this case, the United States kills foreigners who occupy Cambodian territory and does not kill Cambodians." (Deac, 1997, 51).

A large-scale effort to interfere with NVA and Viet Cong infiltration began in November 1969 with the expansion of Highway 246. This fronted on the "Fishhook" -- one of the numerous distinctively-shaped salients in the border between South Vietnam and Cambodia – and already presented an obstacle of open ground where the NVA/VC could be seen and killed. The Americans improved Highway 246 and used Rome Plows to create a vast open space flanking it. Rome Plows, which were massive armored bulldozers built initially in Rome, Georgia, featured a blade with a forward-curved, sharpened lower edge that could slice swiftly through even large trees. The engineers piled and burned the debris, filling the air with smoke but leaving a 1,500 foot wide space of open ground through the jungle, extending from An Loc to Katum. This swath of open ground, cutting through the very areas of Binh Long and Tay Ninh provinces where communist troops crossed the border most heavily, increased NVA/VC casualties further.

Not only did the interdiction start to choke off reinforcements and supplies from Northern guerrillas operating in South Vietnam, but many of the bodies yielded superb intelligence. Some of the bodies found sprawled in Claymore ambush zones, perforated by sudden blasts of steel balls, carried detailed plans, maps, or secret communications, which the Americans collected and deciphered. Additionally, almost all North Vietnamese soldiers and officers kept personal diaries, a cultural peculiarity offering more information to those who killed them. Though generally brief and terse, these diaries helped American and ARVN (Army of South Vietnam) intelligence piece together a picture of the massive scale of Hanoi's operations inside Cambodia. By late 1969, U.S. Military Assistance Command, Vietnam (MACV) came to the conclusion, both from the reports of men in the field and captured documents, that the "tonnages moving through Sihanoukville were sufficient to meet 100 percent of the requirements of enemy units in the... III and IV Corps areas, and perhaps two-thirds of the requirements for enemy units in the II Corps area." (Shaw, 2005, 9). The logistical aspect represented a particular weak point of the

North Vietnamese by 1970. With the Viet Cong, who frequently used captured American weapons and therefore could resupply themselves with ammunition through theft or battlefield capture, nearly extinct, the fighting fell to NVA regular soldiers. However, these men used Soviet and Chinese supplied weapons incompatible with American chambering, and consequently needed every bullet brought in through hostile territory.

The Political Foundations of the Cambodian Campaign

A pair of regime changes ushered in the conditions leading to the Cambodian Campaign, one expected and the other less so. President Lyndon B. Johnson declined to run for a second full term as president, leaving his vice president, Hubert Humphrey, to challenge Republican candidate Richard M. Nixon. Nixon won the election and soon started planning a more aggressive Vietnam strategy. Nixon began by attempting to deal with the North Vietnamese and achieve a peaceful solution. The North Vietnamese government, of course, simply viewed this as a sign of weakness. At one point during their talks with Kissinger, in fact, they candidly informed him of their intention not only to conquer Vietnam but also Laos and Cambodia. Nixon eventually lost patience with the communist state: "After half a year of sending peaceful signals to the Communists, I was ready to use whatever military pressure was necessary to prevent them from taking over South Vietnam by force. During several long sessions, Kissinger and I developed an elaborate orchestration of diplomatic, military, and publicity pressures we could bring to bear on Hanoi." (Prados, 1999, 290).

The second event ushering in the changed strategy involved the leadership of Cambodia. Sihanouk's failure to defeat the Khmer Rouge, his permitting tens of thousands of Vietnamese soldiers to effectively take over eastern Cambodia, and his inability to deal with the rapidly deteriorating economy compelled Prince Sisowath Sirik Matak and Prime Minister Lon Nol to contemplate a coup.

Contemplation became action when Sihanouk took a trip abroad in early 1970, spending several months on the Cote d'Azur and in Paris, ostensibly as a treatment for his obesity and other ailments. His wife Monique accompanied him. In fact, Sihanouk had been helplessly letting the government of his country run into the ground under its own power for several years, interesting himself principally in producing and directing nine widely-mocked films. He left as much to avoid popular unrest over the Vietnamese presence in the country as for his health.

Matters reached a crisis in early March. On March 11th, vast hordes of students, monks, and even police staged demonstrations and marches in Phnom Penh, blazing with rage over the government's refusal to do anything about the growing thousands of communist Vietnamese in the nation. The crowds broke into the North Vietnamese and Viet Cong embassies, looting the buildings, and made a failed attempt on the Chinese embassy.

Sihanouk responded with rage, declaring that he would execute every member of his government when he returned home from Paris. A man who had placed his political enemies in cages before filming their executions, Sihanouk probably could have lived up to his threat. In particular, he loathed Lon Nol utterly, saying of the Prime Minister: "He never understood a damn thing, always stared at me with those ox's eyes and spent all his time praying. Worse, before he blew his nose he would consult the soothsayers to find out whether the stars were favorable for that activity." (Marlay, 1999, 166).

Lon Noi

Prince Sirik Matak probably felt an echo of the same frustration when Lon Nol refused for a time to countenance a coup during Sihanouk's absence. However, the prince eventually convinced the Prime Minister by playing a tape of Sihanouk, sent from Paris by one of his men, in which the king, raging and bellowing, described how he would execute Sirik Matak and Lon Nol along with all the other members of his cabinet.

Rather than returning to deal with the problem immediately, Sihanouk flew to Moscow, hoping to induce the Soviets to pressure the Vietnamese to leave Cambodia. Oum Mannorine, one of Sihanouk's cronies, tried to arrest the two main plotters, but he found himself seized by soldiers instead, to be imprisoned through 1973.

Lon Nol and Sirik Matak took their case to the National Assembly and the High Council of the Kingdom on March 18th, 1970. To their astonishment, a unanimous vote secured Sihanouk's deposition. Though Sihanouk accused the CIA of engineering his fall, the evidence strongly suggests that for a change the organization did not have a hand in events. The South Vietnamese had pledged support, however, and both Lon Nol and Sirik Matak held a pro-Western, pro-American agenda, largely due to their wish to have a powerful ally against the communists both foreign and domestic. The new government called for 10,000 volunteers to expel the communists from eastern Cambodia, and found themselves flooded by 70,000 volunteers instead. Many Cambodians correctly judged communism in general and the Vietnamese in particular to be a threat to their nation and their lives. Unfortunately for the newly minted Khmer Republic, their zealous but drastically inexperienced and under-equipped volunteers proved no match for the flinty professionals of the NVA, or the 12,000 heavily armed Khmer Rouge fighters the North Vietnamese sent back to Cambodia at this time.

Smashed by the communist soldiery, the volunteer force turned their fury on the Vietnamese settlers present in various areas of Cambodia. The volunteers inflicted ghastly retribution on these luckless Vietnamese, many of whom held strongly anticommunist views and eventually fled to South Vietnam.

Lon Nol and Sirik Matak could not control the corruption of Cambodian society and government any more than Sihanouk could. However, they discarded Sihanouk's false neutrality (actually effective collaboration with the North Vietnamese) in favor of turning towards American support. U.S. forces had suddenly gained official permission to openly cross the Cambodian border in strength. Nixon proved willing to hit the North Vietnamese hard in one of their primary 1970 strongholds, and the sudden ascent of the Khmer Republic provided an immediate opportunity to put that desire into action.

The Ground Campaign

A map showing various points of attack across the Cambodian border

The North Vietnamese civilians in Cambodia proved an effective fifth column for the communists following the bloodless coup and establishment of the Khmer Republic. NVA agitators found it easy to stir up large-scale demonstrations and riots among the Vietnamese workers at Cambodia's numerous, extensive rubber plantations.

Lon Nol's government redeployed its troops to quash the Vietnamese riots and Cambodian counter-riots. This enabled the NVA to launch a military offensive in eastern Cambodia which wiped out most of the Cambodian military presence in a strip of land 150 miles long and 9 miles wide along the Cambodia-Vietnam border. They also took six cities, capturing major arsenals at Kratie.

Encouraged by their success, the NVA attacked deeper into Cambodian territory, seizing portions of central Cambodia and almost severing Phnom Penh from its routes to the ocean. The North Vietnamese had begun a systematic conquest of Cambodia in the same manner that they seized portions of Laos, illustrating the truth of Henry Kissinger's sarcastic declaration prior to the Cambodian Campaign: "Who has troops in Cambodia? [...] Not the US. I am impressed again with the linguistic ability of the people of the Indochinese peninsula. We discovered that the Pathet Lao speak Vietnamese, and now we find the same phenomenon in Cambodia." (Drivas, 2001, 142). In the meantime, Creighton Abrams fumed and American leaders in Washington dithered over whether or not to launch an offensive. By this time, Lon Nol openly begged for U.S. or U.N. intervention in his country to preserve it from outright conquest by the North Vietnamese.

The Army of South Vietnam (ARVN) launched the first action of the Cambodian Campaign on April 29th with Toan Thang 42. The ARVN III Corps handled this task, involving an attack into and beyond a large "salient" of the Cambodian border eastward into Vietnam, known as the Parrot's Beak due to its shape on the map.

Securing Highway 1, which ran along the center of the Parrot's Beak in generally east-to-west direction and crossed into Vietnam at a small projection of the border called the Angel's Wing, represented one of Operation Toan Thang 42's initial objectives. Others included repatriating Vietnamese within Cambodia back to their own country, helping Khmer Republic units still operating in the area, and smashing any NVA encountered.

The ARVN proved eager to begin, as previous incursions had alerted the North Vietnamese to the risk of attacks, and they had started shifting their arms and food caches westward, deeper into Cambodia. The ARVN III Corps' brash commander, Lieutenant General Do Cao Tri, would soon earn the sobriquet of "The Patton of the Parrot's Beak" for his successful attack and rapid advance into Cambodia. A tough, hard-driving officer, General Tri benefited from the input of U.S. General Dennis P. McAuliffe, a lieutenant in World War II who served as an adviser to the ARVN during the Vietnam War.

Tri

Time magazine left a vivid description of General Tri, who would die the following year in a helicopter accident, depriving the ARVN of an effective field commander: "At 40, standing 5 ft. 4 in., Tri cuts a figure that is every bit as dashing as his style of command. In addition to his trademark camouflage jungle suit, Tri's combat regalia usually include a black three-starred baseball cap, a snub-nosed Smith & Wesson .38 in a shoulder holster, a leather-covered briar pipe, and a swagger stick carried under the arm. 'I use it to spank the Viet Cong,' Tri says with a wide grin." (Time, 1970, 39).

The attacking force in the Parrot's Beak consisted of four armored cavalry squadrons and four ranger battalions, combined into infantry-armor task forces. The armored cavalry squadrons included two organic III Corps squadrons, plus one apiece from the ARVN 5th and 25th Infantry Divisions, while the rangers hailed from the ARVN 2nd Ranger Group. General Tri organized them into three Task Forces, 225, 318, and 333.

At the end of April, the ARVN Task Forces moved into position along the northern flank of the Parrot's Beak, south of Tay Ninh City. TF 225 and TF 333 would drive southwest across country into the Parrot's Beak, aiming for the towns along Highway 1. To the east, TF 318 would punch along Highway 1 itself, entering Cambodia through the Angel's Wing and then advancing west along the Parrot's Beak center axis.

A picture of ARVN forces in Cambodia

On the morning of April 29th, the ARVN forces opened their attack with an artillery bombardment, along with Vietnamese and American airstrikes, against known or suspected NVA positions. The three task forces then crossed the border into the Parrot's Beak, carrying the fight to the enemy. The ARVN troops proved both elated and vengeful, glad to be on the offensive at last against their hated communist opponents. Captain Raymond Mahoy, riding with the 5th ARVN Cavalry, observed that "the ARVN pretty well ravaged the countryside as we went. Empty homes were often looted of abandoned personal property, cattle and water buffalo herds were transported back across the border, loads of raw rubber were removed, etc. [...] We advisers as a general rule did not agree with this policy, but simply looked upon the practice as a Vietnamese matter." (Nolan, 1990, 75).

Despite the looting, the ARVN plowed forward aggressively through the North Vietnamese lines. The NVA fought back vigorously, defending against the ARVN soldiers from newly built bunker complexes prepared in expectation of an ARVN/American offensive.

Nevertheless, General Tri deployed his forces in a manner reminiscent of George S. Patton, using armor to punch through weakly defended areas and run amok in the NVA rear, while bringing down heavy barrages of artillery and airstrikes against strongpoints. The ARVN overran many caches of supplies, some of them quite large, and took a number of prisoners. The VNAF (South Vietnamese Air Force) used its fleet of Bell UH-1 Iroquois "Huey" helicopters to airlift out prisoners and smaller caches of weaponry and supplies, while leaving larger depots in place for later removal, though under guard. Those that could not be guarded underwent immediate destruction through burning.

On April 29th and 30th, the ARVN killed 84 North Vietnamese and wounded an unknown number at a cost of 16 KIA and 157 WIA. Later in the offensive American UH-1 pilots would find themselves assigned to helicoptering tarpaulins of dead ARVN soldiers and "pieces of them" to South Vietnam for burial.

During Phase I of Operation Toan Thang 42, the ARVN rangers and infantry showed greater fighting spirit and confidence than the armored elements of the Task Forces. Though outfitted with ACAVs and M48 Patton tanks, the South Vietnamese armored cavalry squadrons initially proved reluctant to close with the enemy. Given the high aggression of the rangers and infantry, this often lead to the men on foot spearheading the attacks while the vehicles followed, their crews holding their fire for fear of hitting their own infantry.

The ARVN leaders quickly noted this deficiency and took steps to remedy it. The commanders themselves readily entered the combat zones to get their tardy armored elements moving. General Tri himself took a hand. Throughout the offensive, he flew daily to the operational area, often landing at crisis points to ensure that the attacks went in with proper speed and vigor. His disregard for personal danger took at least one American reporter aback, according to *Time* magazine: "A newsman who joined him on one recent foray was astonished when Tri ordered his helicopter to land virtually in the midst of a skirmish, then ignored vicious Communist rocket and machine gun fire to walk to a tank and order the reluctant driver to attack. 'Go fast, man!' Tri shouted. 'Go fast!'" (Time, 1970, 39).

Every night, Tri flew back to his manor house to spend the evening with his wife and six children, before returning by helicopter early the next morning to fly up and down the lines, landing at multiple points to energize and inspire his men. Soon the ARVN armored units grew in confidence and began operating just ahead of their infantry rather than behind them, serving as a powerful spearhead for assaults.

On May 1st, the ARVN units consolidated their gains. General Tri rotated out two battalions with the heaviest losses and replaced them with a pair of fresh battalions. Then, Phase II of the Operation began on May 2nd with the entry of elements of ARVN IV Corps into the Parrot's Beak from the south. These moved in a pincer movement in coordination with TFs 333 and 225 to crush Base Area 367. Meanwhile, TF 318 continued its drive up Highway 1 to attack the town of Svay Rieng.

General Nguyen Viet Thanh devised most of the operational plan, a successful blueprint which the outspoken Creighton Abrams attributed to the Vietnamese general's intelligence: "The handling of the forces and the tactics of all the forces in IV Corps can only be described as brilliant. [...] General Thanh, the Corps commander – his plan for the assault in the Parrot's Beak was really brilliantly conceived. In fact, he made a lot of the rest of them look like elephants." (Sorley, 1999, 210-211). Like General Tri, General Thanh would soon die in a helicopter accident. The crashes of VNAF UH-1s would deprive the South Vietnamese of two of their most effective, hard-hitting generals – Tri and Thanh – precisely when they needed such men to help stem the NVA tide of the final war years.

As the ARVN forces hit the NVA troops hard in dried-out rice paddies and swaths of jungle, Highway 1 began filling with Vietnamese settlers fleeing back to their country of origin. A vast ribbon of people and oxcarts, powdered with the area's bright red dust, streamed across the border into South Vietnam. American soldiers on the Vietnam side of the border watched these refugees, extracting any who looked like potential NVA infiltrators for interrogation.

IV Corps advanced swiftly and successfully from the south in three combined infantry and armor columns. High mobility and heavy firepower enabled the IV Corps troops to blast their way through all NVA resistance and link up with the III Corps units advancing from the north. By May 5th, organized NVA resistance ended in the Parrot's Beak, though many small groups of North Vietnamese remained at large in the area.

The ARVN forces killed 1,010 NVA in the IV Corps area alone and took 204 prisoners, at a cost of 66 KIA and 330 WIA. The impressive performance of the ARVN helped convince the Americans that handing over the war to the South Vietnamese still represented a viable option for victory.

With the Parrot's Beak secured, the ARVN pulled back temporarily to regroup, while the U.S. 6th Battalion, 31st Infantry Regiment (Polar Bears) and the 3rd Brigade U.S. 9th Division airlifted into the area to hold it as the South Vietnamese prepared for Phase III of Operation Toan Thang 42. Swarms of Iroquois and Apache "Cobra" helicopters filled the sky over the Cambodian province with the whir of rotors as the Americans "hopped" from one spot to another, guided to potential incursions by scouts in Hughes OH-6 Cayuse (informally, "Loach") helicopters.

In the process, the Americans found themselves embroiled in one particularly tough fight in Chantrea, where they discovered a unit of NVA dug in with spiderholes and amid earthen dikes that provided instant field fortifications. Elements of 6/31 Infantry landed there under heavy fire, with Cobra gunships firing at the NVA positions to keep the North Vietnamese heads down, if possible.

The battle for Chantrea continued throughout May 9th and into May 10th. The NVA launched a nighttime attack and the Americans called in Douglas AC-47 Spooky gunships to provide illumination and strafing. The Americans cleared the village by 12 PM, at which point two African-American soldiers nicknamed Tatum and Treetop emptied their weapons into a few of the villagers' water buffaloes, then began trying to set the huts afire. Their officer, furious, stopped them.

The villagers approached and knelt in terror before the Americans, who pulled them to their feet and gave them tinned rations and bars of soap before moving on, to the surprise and relief of the Cambodians, who had never seen U.S. soldiers before. One teenager tried to talk to the soldiers in English, and an old woman warned them in fragmentary French that many Viet Cong were nearby.

The Polar Bears nevertheless pushed forward in pursuit of the NVA soldiers, and met heavy resistance at Ph Tnaot, a forest village with a pagoda. The Americans knocked out several bunkers with hand grenades, pushed in the firing apertures by men in battle-frenzy, and rocket attacks by Cobras. However, they also suffered 8 men killed and 22 wounded by NVA machine gun and mortar fire. The Parrot's Beak remained a lethal zone even after the ARVN smashed the major NVA units there.

American forces in Cambodia in May

After regrouping, the ARVN Task Forces began Phase III of Operation Toan Thang 42. TFs 225 and 318 struck first west out of the neck of the Parrot's Beak into Cambodia proper, then north, roughly parallel with the Cambodia-Vietnam border, beginning on May 7th, 1970. TF 333 functioned as a reserve for the spearhead units.

The two leading Task Forces pushed steadily north, engaging and defeating NVA units in their path and killing close to 200 North Vietnamese during the first day alone. TF 225 took an unoccupied 200-bed NVA hospital and carried off a large cache of high-quality medical and surgical supplies. General Tri led the forces north to the Kompong Spean river by May 9th, an impressive drive of approximately 40 miles in two days.

The ARVN units remained in the Kompong Spean area for several more days, hunting down small NVA units and securing the numerous supply caches and small bases in the area. On May 11th the men received a pair of prominent visitors, South Vietnam's President Nguyen Van Thieu and the nation's Vice President Nguyen Cao Ky. Thieu and Ky toured the units in company with General Tri.

However, Thieu also brought important news to General Tri. Cambodian violence against Vietnamese in and near Phnom Penh escalated swiftly and Thieu wanted his country's citizens evacuated back to their homeland. Accordingly, General Tri received the presidential command to attack along Highway 1 all the way to the Phnom Penh area and secure the road for the escape of the Vietnamese. This represented a much deeper penetration than Nixon authorized, but the South Vietnamese saw little merit in the self-imposed restrictions of the Americans in a total war for their state's survival.

In response to these orders, General Tri fell back to the south, assembling all three Task Forces into a powerful military group on Highway 1. This force jumped off from its starting point at Svay Rieng on May 13th, initiating the operation's Phase IV.

From May 14-21, General Tri's forces engaged and defeated the NVA in a series of encounters in which the ARVN repeatedly won the upper hand. Each battle left dozens of NVA corpses strewn on the field and frequently yielded several dozen prisoners also. This advance brought Tri's men to Kampong Trabek, east of Phnom Penh, and led the ARVN to declare Highway 1 secured for civilian evacuation, though a few Viet Cong attacks continued along the roadway, infuriating General Tri.

At this point, General Tri decided to come to the aid of some Khmer Republic soldiers besieged in the city of Kompong Cham on the Mekong River, some 60 miles north of the Highway 1 axis into Phnom Penh. The communists had continued their attempts to conquer large portions of Cambodia despite the U.S. Army and ARVN attacks across the border, and four understrength Khmer infantry battalions with only four 105mm howitzers in support found themselves trapped by superior NVA forces: "NVA forces for the 9th Division occupied the Chup plantation area northeast of Kompong Cham. They shelled the city and mounted sniper attacks against its eastern part. [...] Communication by way of the Mekong River [...] was also interdicted. The city was then effectively isolated, increasing the problem of food and ammunition shortage. The garrison's morale was at a low ebb; its troops were wondering for how long they could hold under the siege." (Tho, 1979, 65).

Task Forces 333 and 318 moved to the relief of Kompong Cham, joined by additional South Vietnamese forces moving along Route No. 7 and Route No. 15. Converging on the North Vietnamese positions in the huge Chup rubber plantation, the ARVN rangers and armor fought with considerable skill, using their combined arms to defeat the NVA in a series of sharp engagements which led to much higher losses for the North Vietnamese than to their Southern counterparts.

The NVA withdrew on June 1st, giving the city a temporary respite. However, when General Tri pulled back his men for recuperation and refitting, the NVA immediately returned, reoccupied the Chup plantation, and laid siege to Kompong Cham for a second time. From June 21st to June 29th, therefore, the three Task Forces once again attacked the NVA, killing 165 at a cost of 34 KIA and 204 WIA, and once more driving the communist soldiers from the Chup plantation.

By this time, the Cambodian Campaign started winding down, but the ARVN forces, though heavily outnumbered, had killed thousands of NVA soldiers, pushed deep into Cambodia, and seized vast quantities of weapons, ammunition, and rice.

The weapons and ammunition would eventually find their way into the hands of the Khmer Republic's underequipped soldiery, while the South Vietnamese government managed to distribute most of the rice to Vietnamese evacuees from Cambodia, showing a good degree of efficiency in doing so. General Tri could be pleased with the results of Toan Thang 42, which helped set up the possibility for a decisive followup thwarted only by the political situation in the United States.

American Forces and Operation Rockcrusher

A day after General Tri launched Toan Thang 42, the Americans commenced their own attack into Cambodia, Operation Rockcrusher. This operation aimed at another eastward "salient" of the Cambodian border heavily used by communist infiltrators and raiders, the "Fishhook," along with adjacent areas of the frontier. ARVN units also participated in Rockcrusher, but the operation remained chiefly an American expedition under direct U.S. command.

The Americans, pursuant to their orders, would penetrate Cambodian territory only shallowly, remaining much closer to the border than the forces of General Tri to their south. The plan involved inserting Air Cavalry and ARVN airborne units into the Cambodian interior to set up blocking positions behind the forward NVA lines. 15,000-lb "Daisy Cutter" bombs would blast instant landing zones in the thick jungle for these airborne insertions.

An American B52-D dropping bombs

Simultaneously, armored forces would move forward across the border from South Vietnamese territory, serving as the "hammer" crushing the NVA and Viet Cong against the "anvil" of the blocking forces. The Americans hoped to gain complete surprise and thus large numbers of NVA killed or captured, but in reality keeping the setup of such a major operation secret proved impossible. Lieutenant General Michael Davison commanded the Operation Rockcrusher forces overall.

The American units involved consisted mainly of the 1st Cavalry Division (Airborne), also known as the 1st Air Cavalry Division, 1st Air Cav, and First Team. Led at the time by Major General Elvy Roberts, the 1st Air Cavalry featured a unique composition including a fleet 435 helicopters, as compared to the 80 helicopters (or less) of all other American divisions at the time. This gave the First Team unprecedented mobility.

The 11th Armored Cavalry Regiment, known as the Blackhorse Regiment after its unit insignia of a rearing black horse on a diagonally divided red and white field, would also participate, led by George S. Patton, Jr. Lieutenant General Du Quoc Dong led the ARVN Airborne Division, which would assist the 1st Air Cavalry, while the U.S. 25th Infantry Division, Tropic Lightning or more ironically "Electric Strawberry," provided ground forces to support the 11th Armored Cavalry in their "hammer" sweep into Cambodia, under its commander Major General Harris W. Hollis.

General Michael Davison received extremely short notice that he would need to carry out the operation. On April 24th, Creighton Abrams flew to Davison's headquarters at Bien Hoa, and, after lighting up one of the cigars which would soon claim his life with lung cancer, declared, "Mike, I want you to go into Cambodia and clean out those sanctuaries. I want you to do it on seventy-two hours notice; let me know when you're ready." (Coleman, 1991, 221). Though startled and completely new both to his current command and to Vietnam itself, Davison carried out his task with rapid professionalism. The commanders of the units involved, working with

Davison, worked out a plan by April 27th, and shortly thereafter received word they would attack on May 1st. The headquarters finished issuing unit orders on April 30th, immediately before the launch of Rockcrusher. To the south, the ARVN had already engaged.

The Americans let the ARVN attack in the Parrot's Beak first as a diversion, hoping that the North Vietnamese attention would focus there and keep their forces off balance in the Fishhook area. General Creighton Abrams wanted General Tri's ARVN to attack on April 29th, but unfavorable omens from the soothsayers delayed the attack until the following day. General Davison exploded in rage after the liaison with General Tri, according to McAuliffe: "He and the Twenty-fifth ARVN Division [commanding general] dug themselves in and didn't do a damn thing because the stars told them they'd have an exorbitant number of casualties." (Shaw, 2005, 53).

Nevertheless, the American operation began as scheduled. In the predawn darkness of May 1st, 1970, colossal crashes of thunder and glaring bursts of light rolled over the eastern Cambodian jungle just west of the Fishhook as B-52s unleashed their 15,000-lb BLU-82 Daisy Cutter bombs, instantly leveling a series of large clearings in the forest to serve as landing zones (LZ) for the American and ARVN airborne troops. Following this stunning opening, American ground attack aircraft swept in at 6 a.m., at the same time that a powerful howitzer bombardment began, involving approximately 100 tubes. The American attacks targeted known or suspected NVA positions, bunker lines, and strongpoints, attempting to soften up enemy resistance before the H-Hour of 7:30 a.m. Forward air controllers in OV-10 Broncos guided the aircraft to their targets and watched for the expected heavy anti-aircraft fire, but the North Vietnamese did not shoot at the aircraft despite having such weapons available in their stockpiles.

ARVN airborne battalions landed at LZ East (3rd Battalion), Center (5th Battalion), and West (9th Battalion), with streams of UH-1 "Hueys" escorted by Cobras. After earlier thunderstorms, the ground proved wet but practicable for landing, deployment of light artillery pieces, and use of light vehicles. U.S. 2nd Battalion, 7th Cavalry under Lieutenant Colonel Ed Trobaugh landed at LZ XRAY, the fourth landing zone blasted flat by Daisy Cutters a few hours earlier.

Meanwhile, the helicopters of 9th Air Cavalry Squadron crisscrossed the Cambodian train, hunting for NVA troops. The 9th Air Cavalry drew first blood in the Fishhook when 10 NVA riding in the back of a truck made the error of opening fire on the helicopters sweeping over at treetop level, thus drawing the gunners' attention. The Americans fired on the truck, destroying it and killing five of the NVA aboard. Throughout the operational area, NVA fleeing the artillery bombardment found themselves targeted: "1-9th Cavalry had a field day catching small groups of NVA scurrying hither and yon, resulting in a record total of 157 NVA killed by helicopter (on 1 May)." (Phillips, 1999, 66).

In the meantime, the ground forces moved up close to the border to their jumping off points. The men could feel the ground quaking beneath them with the impact of bombs and shells miles away in Cambodian territory. At staggered intervals between 7:30 a.m. and 10 a.m., various elements of the 11th Armored Cavalry rolled across the border and went on the attack.

The 11th Blackhorse men drove their armored columns into the Fishhook area, with M113 ACAVs strengthened by detachments of M48A3 Patton medium tanks and M551 Sheridan light tanks. M109 155mm self-propelled howitzers accompanied each squadron to provide organic fire support for assaults.

On the first day, one squadron of the 11th Armored Cavalry ran into a battalion-strength unit of NVA dug in at the edge of a clearing in the jungle. The NVA killed two Americans, the only U.S. troops to die in Cambodia on May 1st, while the 3rd Squad, 11th Cavalry moved to take them in flank. The 1-9th Air Cavalry arrived to fire at the NVA from the rear, forcing them to abandon their trenches and flee, leaving 52 corpses behind.

The operational plan worked. The ARVN battalions and 2nd Battalion, 7th Cavalry moved out from their Landing Zones and linked up, forming a screen several miles inside Cambodian territory. Like the beaters of a 19th century safari hunt, the 11th Blackhorse and the following elements of 25th Infantry Division "Tropic Lightning" drove the NVA towards the blocking force. Hundreds of North Vietnamese soldiers died and scores more surrendered or found themselves taken prisoner after sustaining wounds.

From the beginning, according to II Field Force commander Lieutenant General Michael Davison, the American soldiers found fresh vigor and motivation in the Cambodian Campaign. Comments to their leaders mostly consisted of variations on two themes: "Why didn't we do this years ago? Why don't the American people understand why we're doing this?" (Sorley, 1999, 206).

In fact, the resistance proved far lighter than the American planners had expected. The local Cambodians told the Americans that hundreds of NVA moved deeper into Cambodia as soon as the preparatory artillery bombardments occurred, though some remained to defend the caches. American engineers prepared additional landing zones and more Air Cavalry troops deployed to help secure the Fishhook and adjacent areas, and to search for weapon and food caches.

By May 3rd, the 11th Armored Cavalry finished clearing their initial objectives. The order now came through to drive 24 miles north to the large town of Snoul, occupied by a force at least 1,000 NVA, according to Cambodian refugees fleeing the communist occupation. Colonel Donn Starry led his 2nd and 3rd Squadron north in a rapid dash along Highway 7 to reach Snoul.

Shortly after noon on May 4th, the armored columns burst out of the jungle into more open country dotted with large rubber plantations. The Americans passed large numbers of Cambodian civilians hurrying south along Highway 7 away from Snoul.

During halts, the U.S. troops gave the civilians C-rations and cigarettes, and some of the Cambodians gave them opened coconuts from which the soldiers drank the coconut milk. The locals told the Americans that the NVA indeed occupied Snoul, but they did not know if any civilians still remained in the settlement.

The communist soldiers had blown the bridges over three small rivers. The Americans bridged the first two easily enough with bridge-laying equipment, but the third proved wider. Even a longer prefabricated span airlifted in by a Hughes XH-17 Flying Crane helicopter proved difficult to install.

Impatient to move ahead, Colonel Starry looked for an alternate crossing (his account referring to himself in the third person): "Anxious not to lose the momentum of the attack, Colonel Starry set out on foot with the section sergeant and the bridge launching vehicle to find a place where the span could be used. After gingerly testing several places, they let down the bridge, tried it out with Troop G, and by 1300 the 2d and 3d Squadrons were again rolling north." (Starry, 2002, 173).

In fact, the span barely extended the full distance, extending only a foot or two onto the crumbling earth of the riverbank on each side. Captain Sewell Menzell crossed in ACAV first, driving the ends of the bridge into the earth and creating a firmer structure. The ACAVs crossed first due to their lighter weight, after which the M48 Patton tanks followed.

When the Americans arrived at Snuol, they found the NVA held the town as described by the civilians. Rather than risk a frontal attack on the town, the 11ᵗʰ Armored Cavalry units attacked through a rubber plantation to take the town's turf airstrip. The NVA had prepared the plantation with fighting positions but aimed their heavy weapons skyward, expecting American "helicopter soldiers" to arrive. This put them at an even heavier disadvantage against the armored vehicles now attacking them.

A furious but short battle erupted as the Americans charged into the plantation: "Instantaneously, the line of Sheridans and ACAVs opened fire into the rubber trees. The racket was such that Menzel couldn't hear a thing through his helmet earphones. All was just a cacophony of bouncing orange tracers and cartwheeling tree branches, dead leaves blasted off the ground, and NVA who were again breaking and running. Menzel saw some NVA fall in the fire and others who stood staring in shock." (Nolan, 1990, 136).

Canister and beehive rounds fired from the tanks' guns blew NVA soldiers to bloody ribbons, and .50 caliber machine gun bullets churned through the rubber trunks and enemy positions. Soon, the NVA fled, abandoning their useless anti-aircraft guns.

During the action, the Americans cornered two North Vietnamese in an ammunition bunker, and at first the NVA soldiers refrained from firing. One man, a lieutenant, soon surrendered, though he muttered a stream of Vietnamese obscenities as he did so. The second man, a private soldier, hurled a grenade out of the bunker, shattering the bones of Major Fred Fields' foot and sending a dozen fragments into Colonel Starry himself. A furious U.S. soldier hurled a grenade back into the bunker, blowing off one arm and one leg of the NVA private. American medics attempted to save the man, but he bled to death swiftly. A medevac helicopter removed Starry and Fields for treatment, and Starry would soon be back in the field.

Pushing into Snuol, the Americans received fire in the central marketplace. They called in airstrikes and artillery, which drove out the NVA but knocked down several buildings and killed four civilians. The North Vietnamese had fired on the Americans precisely to generate anti-American propaganda, and American reporters pounced venomously on this incident to blacken the reputation of their own troops, reporting that the Americans brutally leveled the entire town. In fact, the NVA had already destroyed a number of buildings near the central marketplace during their conquest of the town a few weeks earlier. Most of the commercial buildings still stood even after the American bombardment, and the entire residential section remained undamaged, but the American press nevertheless harped endlessly on a nonexistent obliteration of Snuol.

Strictly limited on the depth of penetration allowed, the Americans had already reached and in some cases gone beyond their politically mandated operational boundaries. Accordingly, the 11ᵗʰ Armored Cavalry withdrew and let the infantry take over the process of searching out and capturing or destroying the caches of the North Vietnamese. One of the biggest coups consisted of taking "The City," a colossal complex including hundreds of buildings and storage sheds, training facilities, 18 mess halls, and barracks, covering an area about 1.5 miles long and a mile wide. The Americans retrieved an immense trove of stores, including, "1,282 individual weapons; 202 crew-served weapons; 319,000 rounds of 12.7-mm ammunition; 25,200 rounds of 14.5-mm antiaircraft ammunition; 1,555,900 rounds of AK-47 ammunition; 2,110 hand grenades; 58,000 lbs. of explosives; 400,000 rounds of caliber .30 machine gun ammunition; 22 crates of anti-personnel mines; 30 tons of rice; 8 tons of corn; 1,100 lbs. of salt." (Tho, 1979, 77).

The astonished GI's also found superb living quarters for officers (despite the alleged egalitarianism of the communists) surrounded by manicured lawns, several large swimming pools, a firing range, and pens containing pigs and chickens. The troops greeted the discovery of a cache of hundreds of brand-new, completely unused SKS 7.62mm semi-automatic carbines, fully legal in the United States, unlike the automatic AK-47. The American soldiers took most of these rifles to bring back with them to the U.S. as loot.

The rest of the materiel took weeks to extract, even with the help of ARVN labor battalions. Once again, the South Vietnamese government distributed most of the rice to Vietnamese and Cambodian refugees. Those weapons not claimed by American souvenir hunters, along with most of the ammunition, found its way to the Khmer Republic forces in Cambodia to use in their struggle against the Khmer Rouge and NVA.

A picture of Cambodian civilians bagging up captured rice

The Americans used a variety of methods for ferreting out the numerous additional caches of the NVA and Viet Cong. While some base and sanctuary areas could not be missed, many others featured extremely careful concealment. The U.S. troops tried using Cambodian advisers, North Vietnamese prisoners, and even enlisted technology in the search, as General Davison's debriefing report described: "We even resorted to the Navy's magnetic anomaly detectors, and conscientiously followed up on readings by the "Iron Barnacle", as the US 25th Infantry Division referred to this Navy gear. However, the instrument was too sensitive and would pick up empty C-ration and beer cans; consequently, only 10 percent of the readings proved fruitful." (Davison, 1971, 20).

While the Americans and ARVN stumbled across some caches using these techniques, men who developed a "sixth sense" for the hidden supply dumps located most of the materiel found during Operation Rockcrusher. These experienced units developed an intuitive way of finding NVA caches based on their knowledge of how the North Vietnamese hid their gear and foodstuffs, along with observation of the local terrain, the pattern of NVA trails, and other signs of human activity. The NVA and Viet Cong also inadvertently betrayed the location of a number of their caches. They tended to slip away when they had nothing to defend and put up resistance when the Americans neared a cache. Therefore, the U.S. troops soon learned that coming under fire meant that a cache probably lay close by and that a detailed search might well yield results after winning the firefight. Had the NVA left their caches undefended fewer would have been found, perhaps far fewer.

Late in the operation, Davison thought to bring in Rome Plows to clear the jungle from tracts of ground where his men suspected that buried or hidden stores lay. This method proved highly effective where used, but since Davison did not think of the idea until a few days before the American withdrawal, time constraints greatly limited the total "haul" from Rome Plow operations.

Furthermore, the Rome Plows required escort from armored forces rather than infantry. Early attempts to use the powerful bulldozers with infantry support led to the men on foot rapidly falling behind the Rome Plows, exposing them to B40 rocket attacks and other assaults by the North Vietnamese. Rome Plow operator casualties dropped immediately when the Americans deployed ACAVs or M551 Sheridans to guard them.

The offensive met with the approval of most of the men participating in it. Instead of being forced into the passive role of responding to the North Vietnamese, and suffering the frustration of countless nitpicking restrictions, the American troops now found themselves taking constructive action and carrying the fight to the enemy. This boosted morale, and Creighton Abrams reported that "they have reacted well to attacking the enemy in his secure sanctuaries. American troops always feel better when they are on the offensive. Not only the soldiers, but also the leaders at all levels, have taken the initiative in getting the job done." (Sorley, 1999, 206).

Even the brief, limited incursion into Cambodia had produced startling results, indicating that even greater success and, quite possibly, a war-winning knockout blow could have resulted if the military had been allowed to continue smashing the communist invaders in Cambodia and Laos. The North Vietnamese lost 11,349 soldiers killed, and the U.S. Army and ARVN took 2,328 prisoners. The logistical effects proved even larger. The Americans and ARVN destroyed or captured at least 305 trucks, a sizable transport pool. They also took enough ammunition to supply every current combat battalion of the North Vietnamese Army then in the field for 6 months and enough rice to feed those same units for an entire year.

At this point, however, politics intervened drastically in the operations. Edward Kennedy led a group of other representatives in an almost frenzied attack on the Cambodian Campaign. The press, filled with outrage, blasted Nixon's administration for "expanding the war," even though the North Vietnamese had already begun brutally conquering those portions of Cambodia and Laos most useful to them, while openly announcing their intention to seize both nations to add to their Indochinese communist empire.

Ted Kennedy

The crisis of massive student demonstrations, during which National Guard troops killed four protestors at Kent State in May 1970, finally placed sufficient pressure on the Nixon administration to bring the ground campaign to a halt. American forces began withdrawing in June, and by June 30th, only ARVN units remained in Cambodia. The Americans even pulled their advisers back inside Vietnam's borders. However, American forces would continue to participate somewhat in the effort to break up the communist logistical networks in Cambodia and Laos. Though the ground forces had withdrawn, the air campaign continued into late 1970.

The Air Campaign

American bombing runs actually preceded the ground invasion of the 1970 Cambodian Campaign, and clandestine airstrikes, bombing, and hunter-killer missions continued after the official U.S. withdrawal on June 30th.

Initially, the North Vietnamese responded aggressively to the Cambodian Campaign. In a rough sense, the opponents of the Presidential policy on Cambodia spoke the truth when they stated that the intervention escalated the situation there. Where they erred lay in a naive faith that peace would prevail in the country if not for the Americans. Lon Nol and the NVA had already come to blows before the Americans crossed the border, and the North Vietnamese had gone on the offensive (and continued it for some time, disregarding the border incursion) into central Cambodia prior to Toan Thang 42 or Rockcrusher. However, the incursion led the North Vietnamese to feed more troops into the theater, precisely as strategy would dictate if they did not intend to cease operations there (as they did not). These troops entered Cambodia along the roads, rivers, and trails in the country's northeastern provinces.

American reconnaissance aircraft cast a wide net over the Cambodian landscape, far beyond the limits of the ground incursion, and soon detected the inflow of North Vietnamese troops. With both photographic and verbal confirmation of the NVA reinforcements, the American command decided to attack these forces from the air. The U.S. 7th Air Force would carry out many of these missions, but hunter-killer helicopter teams from the 1-9th Cavalry (of the 1st Air Cavalry Division) and other air cavalry squadrons also played an important role throughout the rest of 1971.

These strikes against North Vietnamese reinforcements, and additional strikes against NVA engaged in combat with Cambodian forces attempting to defend their country, fell under the umbrella of "Operation Freedom Deal." Freedom Deal initially aimed at a swath of northeast Cambodia bounded by the South Vietnamese border on the east, a line 200 yards west of the Mekong River on the west, the Laotian border on the north, and Highway 13 on the south.

Despite being hammered from the air, the NVA continued determinedly attacking and seizing Cambodian towns and territory. They soon threatened the important regional towns of Bakiev, Labansiek, and Lomphat. With the fall of these towns imminent, the 7th Air Force requested wider powers of interdiction and an expanded operational area. The Joint Chiefs of Staff issued an authorization on June 17th "to employ U.S. tactical air interdiction in any situation which involves a serious threat to major Cambodian positions such as a provincial capital whose loss would constitute a serious military or psychological blow to the country." (Hartsook, 2012, 91).

The Americans soon added a large band of territory west of the Mekong River to the operational area, dubbing this Freedom Deal Alpha. After the June 30th withdrawal of U.S. ground forces into South Vietnam, command added a second extension to the Freedom Deal area southward, encompassing the Fishhook and Dog's Head areas and ending at the northern edge of the Parrot's Beak.

Freedom Deal allowed the use of powerful bombing attacks by B-52s, provided that these occurred at least 0.6 miles (1 kilometer) from the nearest inhabited village and 1.8 miles (3 kilometers) from the closest friendly troops (ARVN, U.S., or Khmer Republic). The rules of engagement allowed attacks on trucks and speedboats, since these vehicles and craft almost certainly belonged to the enemy, Cambodian villagers being far too poor to possess either or even learn how to operate them.

Other restrictions also applied. The 7th Air Force identified buildings of historical value and forbade bombing or airstrikes near them unless by explicit Cambodian invitation. The Americans also tried to distribute leaflets and use loudspeakers to warn civilians away from areas where they planned a bombing attack.

The U.S. government clearly telegraphed its intention to use air power even more heavily in Cambodia after the ground withdrawal. As Secretary of State William P. Rogers told Murrey Marder of the *Washington Post* during a June 25th, 1970 news conference: "After our troops leave Cambodia, our Air Force will be used, be permitted, to interdict the supply lines and communication lines in Cambodia... It is obvious, of course, that there will be times when this will be of direct benefit to the present government in Cambodia." (Niehaus, 1973, 49).

Rogers

Though the monsoon season cut back sharply on the number of sorties per month until it eased, the U.S. air campaign in Cambodia stepped up nevertheless. In the second half of 1970, during Operation Freedom Deal, the share of U.S. air assets in the Vietnam theater committed to Cambodia rose from 8% to 15%. The Americans intended for this strategy, in part, to compensate for the drawdown of their numbers occurring due to Vietnamization. Shifting a greater percentage aircraft and sorties to Cambodia kept up the pressure even as the overall absolute total of airplanes slowly declined. However, they also wished to continue the evident success of the ground portion of the Cambodian Campaign, even though, in practice, the most lethal array of airstrikes and bombing runs could not produce the solid gains of "boots on the ground."

The hunter-killer Pink Teams from 1ˢᵗ Air Cavalry Division – mostly 1-9th Air Cavalry – provided a means of carrying out operations quite similar to armored vehicle sweeps. Each team consisted of two helicopters, a QH-6A Loach scouting helicopter with a three-man crew, and an AH-1 Cobra gunship. Flying out of Tay Ninh, these missions generally remained within 20 miles of the frontier but sometimes reached the Mekong.

In hunting through an area, the AH-1 Cobra remained at 2,000 feet, while the Loach made a quick survey of the zone to spot roads, trails, and possible NVA concentrations. The Loach then dropped lower and followed the trails like a vehicle, hovering approximately 3 to 5 feet off the ground. Warrant Officer Mark Hilton later described how a Loach crew operated: "You almost became one with your environment [...] You could sense people out there in the bush. Even if you didn't see evidence of people, you always knew they were there." (Morrocco, 1985, 85).

Once the Loach made contact it would immediately dart upward, while one of the crew popped smoke both to cover its retreat and provide the lurking AH-1 with an exact fix on the NVA. The Cobra then swooped in, unleashing a hail of cannon fire, shooting its rockets, and firing its minigun as required. The pair of helicopters called in fighter-bomber airstrikes in the event of a supply cache or large NVA unit.

American aircraft provided close air support to Khmer Republic forces defending against the North Vietnamese invaders or, in some cases, launching offensives of their own. The NVA launched a heavy attack on the city of Kampong Thom starting on June 4th, attempting to seize it from Cambodian Republic defenders. The NVA made slow but dangerous progress against the city, until MACV authorized airstrikes in support of the Cambodian troops on June 20th.

The number of sorties remained modest – only 82 fighter sorties between June 20th and June 30th – but the arrival of the American airmen immediately changed the tide of battle. With NVA positions and attacking forces shattered by U.S. strikes, the Cambodians forced the North Vietnamese to retreat, retaining control of Kampong Thom for the time being. Lon Nol was enthused, saying, with a touch of exaggeration, "The image of the aircraft of your 7th Air Force has been solidly anchored since the 20th of June, historical date of the city of Kompong Thom, in the spirits of all the fighters of this city, who owe their survival and their [being] to the action of these aircraft which allowed the solid rise of their morale and stopped any more deaths." (Hartsook, 2012, 92).

During Freedom Deal, the 7th Air Force found itself constrained in the number of sorties it could mount. With the aircraft and crews available, the total number of sorties could actually have ranged much higher. However, the amount of ordnance each month's defense budget allocated to the 7th put a hard limit on its offensive capability. That said, the 7th Air Force found itself able to "bank" unused ordnance in months of poor weather, allowing higher sortie totals once meteorological conditions improved.

Freedom Deal became Freedom Action in July, but the basic outline of the operation remained the same. In order to squeeze the maximum amount of effect out of their limited sorties, the Air Force studied the results of the many different kinds of aircraft involved closely. They came to the conclusion that Lockheed AC-130A Spectre gunships represented the most efficient destroyers of NVA men and materiel, but that its low operating altitude meant that it could only be used on nights with less than 50% illumination from the moon. It also needed McDonnell Douglas F-4 Phantom II interceptor fighters to handle anti-aircraft artillery and similar threats.

The Americans did not always respond to Cambodian requests for air support, instead frequently relying on their own analysis of the situation to decide whether to intervene in a given battle. If they believed the Cambodians could win on their own, they usually refrained from sending aircraft. However, if the situation appeared dangerous, they would send gunships, fighter-bombers, and in some cases flareships to provide illumination to help with repelling NVA night attacks.

Moreover, the 7th Air Force did not always execute only standard combat missions. A number of missions using C-7 Caribou STOL (Short Takeoff and Landing) transport aircraft evacuated a considerable number of refugees, plus their portable possessions, from eastern Cambodia's war zones to South Vietnam. There the South Vietnamese fed them from the bounty of rice seized from the NVA during the Cambodian Campaign itself.

A less pacific mission involved the deployment of magnetic mines in the San and Kong Rivers, starting in the first week of June 1970. Aircraft dropped some 1,600 of these devices into the waters of these Mekong tributaries, used heavily by the NVA to bring supplies south to the forces fighting to defeat Lon Nol's government. Their advantage lay in the fact that metal hulled boats detonated them, meaning that local civilians, invariably in possession of wooden hulled boats, could pass directly over them without coming to harm.

After the mines blew a number of their steel-hulled speedboats to pieces, the NVA quickly adapted to this new hazard. They simply seized wooden hulled boats and used those in place of the speedboats. The mines still presented a slight risk, however, since the metal in an outboard motor fitted to a wooden hull still sometimes set them off. To put an end to the threat, the NVA tied empty steel drums together into large rafts and floated these down the current. The rafts detonated the mines, effectively sweeping the rivers.

While the Americans handled the lion's share of airstrikes and bombing in Cambodia, the air forces of Vietnam (VNAF) and Cambodia also played a role in striking at the communist soldiery swarming through the countryside. The tiny Cambodian air force attempted sorties, even though its small size, almost total lack of spare parts, and poor pilot training placed strong limits on its effectiveness. The Cambodians fielded 12 MiG-17s inherited from Sihanouk at the start of the Cambodian Campaign. However, after a few months, these had expended all their Soviet ordnance. With no fresh supplies arriving from now-hostile Russia, the Cambodians permanently grounded their MiG-17s.

However, the Americans supplied the Cambodians with 14 North American T-28 Trojan close-support aircraft. These piston-engined aircraft flew about 12 sorties daily during the summer and autumn of 1970, and the Cambodians occasionally launched 18 sorties during particularly critical encounters.

While the Cambodians kept up their brave but relatively puny effort, the VNAF of South Vietnam put in a considerably more robust appearance in Cambodia. The main combat aircraft of the VNAF remained the piston-engined Douglas A-1 Skyraider until relatively late in the war. Nevertheless, as Colonel Peter van Brussel pointed out, the VNAF enjoyed the services of a highly experienced cadre of pilots: "I've got 300 combat flying hours [...] That's a respectable amount for a U.S. pilot but hardly a start for Vietnamese airmen. Many of the men I work with have more than 3,000." (Morrocco, 1985, 85).

Though the South Vietnamese pilots possessed immense experience, they lacked both numbers and training in the more advanced aircraft the Americans started giving them in 1969-1970. The United States provided Cessna A-37 Dragonfly light ground attack jets, Northrop F-5A Freedom Fighter supersonic jet fighters, AC-47 Spooky gunships, and Fairchild AC-119 gunships. The Americans also started the training of 6,000 South Vietnamese technicians who could maintain and repair all these aircraft.

Additionally, the ARVN troops used UH-1 helicopters for transport, acting as "helicopter soldiers" in their own right. This, of course would soon prove costly to them when Generals Tri and Thanh died in helicopter crashes, depriving the South Vietnamese of two of their best commanders.

The Americans launched 14,600 sorties during Rockcrusher, while the VNAF undertook 9,600. However, coordination remained poor between the South Vietnamese and Cambodians, due to the latter's distrust of the former. Additionally, the Cambodians proved notably less capable of using modern aircraft professionally, as the adviser Lieutenant Colonel Paul Wagoner observed: "They want to fight the war their way, by themselves [...] [but] It will surprise me if the AOCC [air operations coordination center] works effectively without U.S. influence [...] I feel we must help them all we can." (Nalty, 2000, 210).

During this time, the Americans also constructed airbases and runways for the South Vietnamese to assist with the process of "Vietnamization." While the Americans pounded the NVA heavily in Cambodia, matters would soon be handed over entirely to the local military. Operation Freedom Action therefore became an opportunity for the allies to work together and the South Vietnamese to learn the methods of carrying on air war from their highly proficient American allies.

The Americans continued to surpass the South Vietnamese in many areas of aerial combat, including nocturnal operations and flying in adverse weather conditions, but a visible improvement occurred nevertheless. One unknown American officer observed in a February 1971 report on the VNAF, "The Vietnamese pilots cannot be surpassed. Time and time I've watched them drop precisely where the FAC [forward air controller] directed. And in this kind of war, where allied and enemy troops are often separated by only a few yards, absolute precision is required." (Hartsook, 2012, 146-147).

Due to strictly limited manpower, the VNAF faced a tradeoff between actually flying and receiving additional training. The choice devolved ultimately to having their pilots in the air or in the classroom. Nevertheless, their tactical control abilities grew steadily, especially towards the end of 1970, when the Americans began to drastically step down the number of missions flown.

The number of American missions dropped precipitously in October 1970, bringing the main air campaign in Cambodia to a close. Though U.S. pilots would continue to operate over Cambodia and Laos, the theater now belonged more to the ARVN and VNAF than to the United States. American attention eventually shifted to North Vietnam, where the Americans used air attacks to coerce the release of prisoners still held and tortured by the North Vietnamese.

The effects of the Cambodian air campaign remain less quantifiable than those of the ground campaign. Though the Americans and VNAF succeeded in destroying some convoys, intelligence noted sourly that pilots always greatly exaggerated the damage they inflicted when no on-the-ground data existed to contradict them. This, in fact, has been true of all air forces in every war during which aircraft saw use.

At the very least, the American attacks proved tactically useful to the Cambodians in their struggle to defeat the Khmer Rouge and the North Vietnamese, but insufficient to turn the tide in a war where the amateur forces of Cambodia could not resist the more professional communist armies in the long run. The Cambodian Campaign itself, however, did at least provide the Cambodian Republic with large amounts of seized NVA weapons and ammunition with which to carry on the struggle.

The Effects of the Cambodian Campaign

From a strictly military viewpoint, without considering whether or not the United States should have fought the Vietnam War in the first place, the Cambodian Campaign of 1970 represented a considerable tactical success. The losses of NVA manpower, though considerable, paled beside the crippling blow delivered to North Vietnamese supplies by the seizure or destruction of NVA caches and the closure of the Sihanoukville Trail.

Indicators that the Americans and ARVN devastated the North's logistics for some time include the sharp drop-off in attacks against Americans in South Vietnam during 1971 and 1972. While Vietnamization meant that the number of American troops declined steadily as the Army brought them home, the fall in attacks outpaced this draw-down by a hefty margin, indicating a lack of attackers rather than lack of targets.

Those NVA still operating in the south soon found themselves starving and lacking ammunition to carry on the struggle. In late 1970 and 1971, American units in South Vietnam began reporting NVA following them, not to attack but to scavenge their garbage for still-edible remnants of food. When confronted, these NVA typically fled after firing a few or no shots, trying to retain their last few bullets.

Some parallel exists between the 1970 Cambodian Campaign and the Tet Offensive. The Tet Offensive backfired on the communists, leading to their relentless destruction in detail by U.S. forces once the latter recovered from the initial shock of the attack. This placed the Americans in a position to smash the North Vietnamese utterly and end the war in their favor, but politics created barriers the Americans could not overcome and the chance for victory slipped away, squandered by political inability to stomach striking a decisive blow.

In a similar way, albeit on a slightly more modest scale, the Cambodian Campaign placed the Americans suddenly in a temporary position of martial dominance. They had destroyed the logistical basis for North Vietnamese military operations in South Vietnam for at least a year and possibly longer. Had this been used as a springboard for further offensives in Cambodia and Laos, the strong possibility exists the U.S. Army could have eliminated any chance of a communist victory in the South, even without invading North Vietnam proper. But once again, politics intervened, and the Americans, casting away the successes of the Cambodian Campaign, continued their retreat – defeated not by the North Vietnamese, but by their own press and politicians.

Bibliography

Caputo, Philip, *A Rumor of War*, 1988.

Coleman, J.D. *Incursion: From America's Chokehold on the NVA Lifelines to the Sacking of the Cambodian Sanctuaries.* New York, 1991.

Davison, Michael S., and Jack P. Cook. *Senior Officer Debriefing Report – Lieutenant General Michael S. Davison.* Washington, D.C., June 9th 1971.

Deac, Wilfred P. *The Road to the Killing Fields: The Cambodian War of 1970-1975.* College Station, 1997.

Drivas, Peter G. "The Cambodian Incursion Revisited." *International Social Science Review.* Volume 86, Nos. 3&4, June 1st, 2011, pp. 134-159.

Hartsook, Elizabeth, and Stuart Slade. *Air War Vietnam: Plans and Operations, 1969-1975.* Newtown, 2012.

Marlay, Russ and Clark Neher. *Patriots & Tyrants: Ten Asian Leaders.* Lanham, 1999.

Morrocco, John. *Rain of Fire: Air War, 1969-1973.* Boston, 1985.

Nalty, Bernard C. *Air War over South Vietnam, 1968-1975.* Washington, D.C., 2000.

Niehaus, Marjorie. "DS 558 C2 '1' 73-114 F: United States Policy Toward Cambodia April 1970 - June 1973: Statements by President Nixon. Dr. Henry Kissinger, and the Secretaries of State and Defense." *Library of Congress Congressional Research Service.* Washington, D.C., June 30th, 1973.

Nolan, Keith William. *Into Cambodia: Spring Campaign, Summer Offensive, 1970*. Novato, 1990.

Phillips, Donald V. *Across the Border: The Successes and Failures of Operation Rockcrusher*. Fort   Leavenworth, 1999.

Prados, John. *The Blood Road: The Ho Chi Minh Trail and the Vietnam War*. New York, 1999.

Shaw, John M. *The Cambodian Campaign. The 1970 Offensive and America's Vietnam War*. Lawrence, 2005.

Sorley, Lewis. *A Better War: The Unexamined Victories and Final Tragedy of America's Last Years in Vietnam*. Orlando, 1999.

Starry, Donn A. *Mounted Combat in Vietnam*. Washington, D.C., 2002.

Summers, Col. Harry G., *On Strategy: A Critical Analysis of the Vietnam War*, 1984.

Tho, Tran Dinh. *The Cambodian Incursion*. Washington, D.C., 1979.

Time Magazine staff. "The Patton of the Parrot's Beak." *Time*. Volume 95, Issue 23, p. 39; 6/8/1970.

Willenson, Kim, *The Bad War: an Oral History of the Vietnam War*, 1987.

Young, Marilyn B. *The Vietnam Wars, 1945 – 1990*, 1990.

Free Books by Charles River Editors

We have brand new titles available for free most days of the week. To see which of our titles are currently free, click on this link.

Discounted Books by Charles River Editors

We have titles at a discount price of just 99 cents everyday. To see which of our titles are currently 99 cents, click on this link.

Made in the USA
San Bernardino, CA
20 August 2019